Sports Illustrated KIDS

Mascot Mania

# HOCKEY'S WEIRDEST MASCOTS:

## FROM AL THE OCTOPUS TO VICTOR E. GREEN

BY DAVID CARSON

Published by Capstone Press, an imprint of Capstone.
1710 Roe Crest Drive North Mankato, Minnesota 56003
capstonepub.com

Library of Congress Cataloging-in-Publication Data is available on the Library of Congress website.
ISBN: 9781666347197 (hardcover)
ISBN: 9781666353228 (ebook PDF)

Summary: Hockey fans are thrilled by last-second slap shots and the horn that signals a winning score. But along with the action on the ice, fans love the strange but loveable mascots that entertain them in the stands. From a big, fluffy moose that pumps up the crowd to a huge purple octopus that drops to the ice before playoff games, fans enjoy the silly stunts and goofy antics of hockey's weirdest mascots!

Editorial Credits
Editor: Aaron Sautter; Designer: Terri Poburka; Media Researcher: Morgan Walters;
Production Specialist: Polly Fisher

Image Credits
Getty Images: Al Bello, 22, Brian Babineau, spread 18-19, Bruce Bennett, 6, 12, Dave Reginek, spread 26-27, Icon Sportswire, 10, spread 20-21, Justin K. Aller, spread 8-9, Len Redkoles, spread 16-17, Tom Pennington, spread 14-15; Newscom: Matthew Pearce/Icon Sportswire 169, bottom left Cover; Shutterstock: Adam Vilimek, spread 4-5; Sports Illustrated: David E. Klutho, top Cover, bottom right Cover, middle right Cover, spread 24-25, spread 28-29

# Table of CONTENTS

# GAME TIME!

Life as a hockey mascot isn't easy. They have to know how to skate. And they have to keep fans entertained at the **arena** night after night. But it's all worth it. These colorful characters know how to get the crowd pumped up for game time!

All sorts of mascots are found throughout the National Hockey League (NHL). They come in all shapes and sizes. Some are adorable and cuddly. Others are wacky and weird. They can be animals, aliens, or something completely strange.

Whatever they look like, hockey mascots know how to heat things up for fans. With t-shirt cannons, cool dance moves, and lots of **selfies** with the fans, it's all part of the game for hockey mascots!

# SPARKY THE DRAGON

Don't let his big, sharp teeth fool you. Sparky the Dragon is as friendly as can be. This silly monster is the official mascot of the New York Islanders. He's big. He's blue. And he loves having fun at the hockey rink.

Why do the Islanders have a dragon mascot? For many years Sparky was the mascot for the New York Dragons. The Dragons were a football team that played in the same arena as the Islanders. Sparky was a big hit with the fans. So when the football team went out of business, Sparky just moved over to the Islanders. It was meant to be!

Before the puck drops, Sparky skates around the rink with a giant team flag to pump up the fans. He sometimes makes exciting entrances too. He's known for being lowered onto the ice from the arena's ceiling. What a crazy stunt!

### Did You Know?

Sparky used to wear two sets of colors, depending on which team he was cheering for.

### ★ STATS ★

**NAME:**
Sparky the Dragon

**HOME TEAM:**
New York Islanders

**FIRST APPEARANCE:**
2010

**FUN FACT:**
Sparky's tail is actually in the shape of a hockey stick.

# GNASH

With his big, toothy smile, Gnash is a big hit. His family history goes way back. In 1971, a construction crew discovered ancient bones of a sabre-tooth cat beneath the city. These big, fierce cats had huge teeth and lived thousands of years ago during the last **ice age**.

Years later, Gnash was discovered during the construction of the Nashville Predators' stadium. He was found encased in ice. He'd been frozen for thousands of years! When Gnash thawed out, he became the Predators' official mascot.

These days Gnash is right at home prowling around the icy hockey rink. During home games he loves to dance and take selfies with his youngest fans. He even performs crazy stunts on his 4-wheeler.

**Did You Know?**

Gnash isn't the NHL's only saber-toothed mascot. "Sabretooth" is the mascot for the Buffalo Sabres.

**★ STATS ★**

**NAME:**
Gnash

**HOME TEAM:**
Nashville Predators

**FIRST APPEARANCE:**
1998

**FUN FACT:**
Gnash often makes his entrance by dropping down a rope from the stadium rafters while the team's theme music blasts over the loudspeakers.

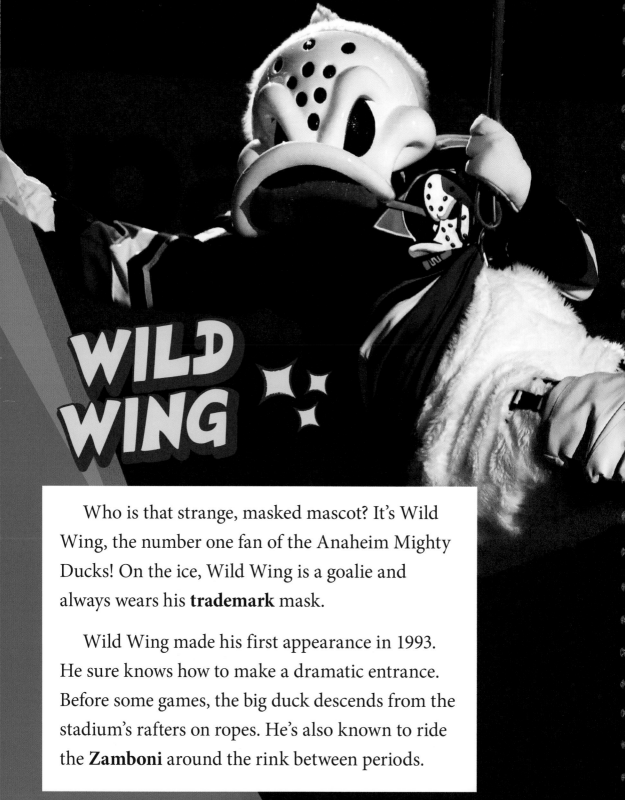

# WILD WING

Who is that strange, masked mascot? It's Wild Wing, the number one fan of the Anaheim Mighty Ducks! On the ice, Wild Wing is a goalie and always wears his **trademark** mask.

Wild Wing made his first appearance in 1993. He sure knows how to make a dramatic entrance. Before some games, the big duck descends from the stadium's rafters on ropes. He's also known to ride the **Zamboni** around the rink between periods.

During the game Wild Wing loves dancing in the stands with his fans. On his days off, Wild Wing visits schools and hospitals in the Anaheim area.

## MASCOT MOVIE STAR

The Anaheim Ducks logo and mascot are based on the 1992 hit movie *The Mighty Ducks.* The Disney Company originally owned the team. Wild Wing was later featured in a cartoon version of *The Mighty Ducks.* In the cartoon, Wild Wing is a muscular superhero.

★ STATS ★

**NAME:**
Wild Wing

**HOME TEAM:**
Anaheim Mighty Ducks

**FIRST APPEARANCE:**
1993

**FUN FACT:**
Wild Wing's favorite songs are *Rock the Pond* and *Wild Thing.*

CARLTON THE BEAR

TORONTO MAPLE LEAFS

★ STATS ★

**NAME:**
Carlton the Bear

**HOME TEAM:**
Toronto Maple Leafs

**FIRST APPEARANCE:**
1995

**FUN FACT:**
Carlton gets his name and jersey number from the home address of the team's longtime home at Maple Leaf Gardens: 60 Carlton St.

Look at that cuddly bear roaming the ice rink. It's Carlton the Bear! He's the official mascot of the Toronto Maple Leafs. Carlton is an adorable polar bear who loves giving his fans giant bear hugs.

Carlton always works hard to entertain Leafs fans. Over the years Carlton has tossed more than 15,000 **souvenir** t-shirts into the crowd. And fans love to cheer along with Carlton as he bangs his drum to pump up his team for victory.

Sometimes Carlton gets to hit the road with his favorite team too. He's appeared in more than 20 other NHL stadiums to cheer on the Maple Leafs.

# VICTOR E. GREEN

He's big. He's fuzzy. He's an alien. He's Victor E. Green—the official mascot for the Dallas Stars. With his pot belly and googly eyes, Victor is a big hit with the fans.

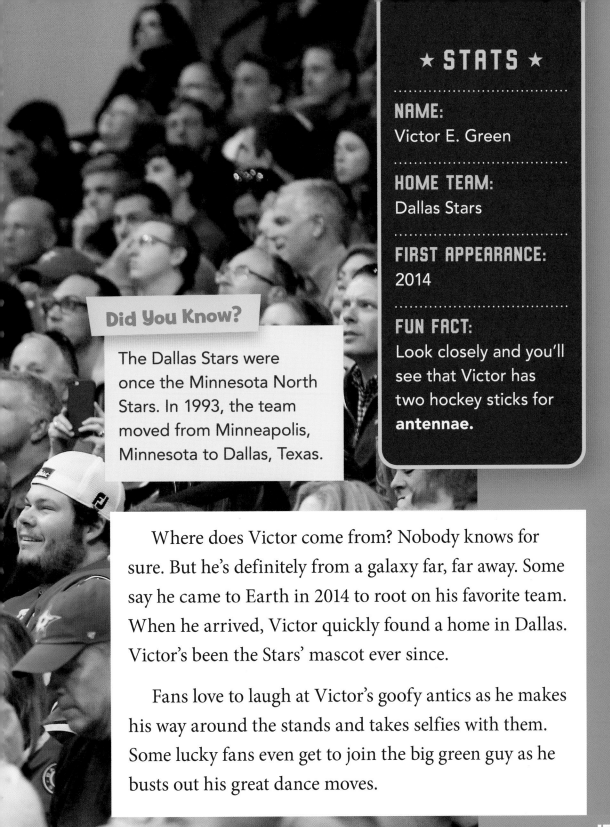

**Did You Know?**

The Dallas Stars were once the Minnesota North Stars. In 1993, the team moved from Minneapolis, Minnesota to Dallas, Texas.

Where does Victor come from? Nobody knows for sure. But he's definitely from a galaxy far, far away. Some say he came to Earth in 2014 to root on his favorite team. When he arrived, Victor quickly found a home in Dallas. Victor's been the Stars' mascot ever since.

Fans love to laugh at Victor's goofy antics as he makes his way around the stands and takes selfies with them. Some lucky fans even get to join the big green guy as he busts out his great dance moves.

# GRITTY

9:59 PM

6 7 3
15 10

For a Complete List of UPCOMING EVENTS
at the Wells Fargo Center, please visit...

## Did You Know?

According to legend,
Gritty was living in a
cave below the Flyers'
stadium before joining
the team as its mascot.

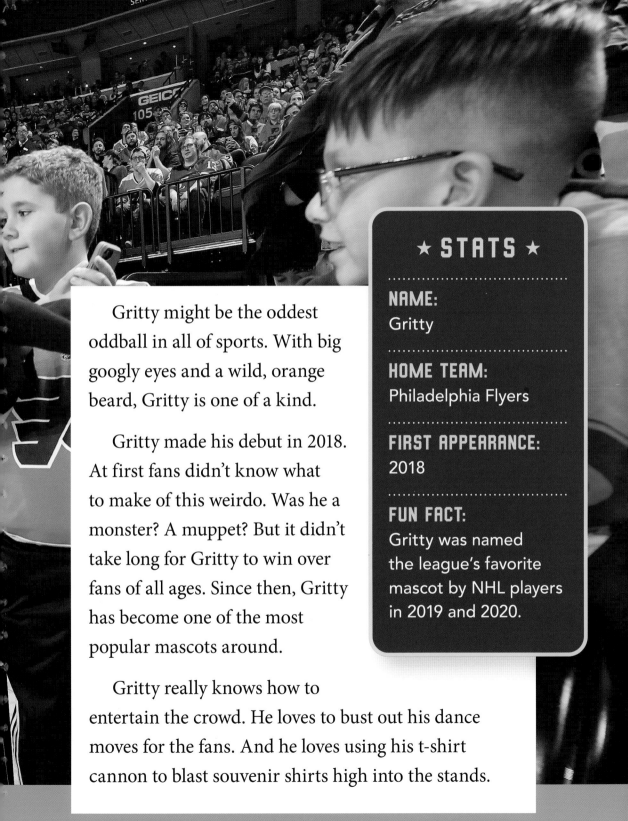

Gritty might be the oddest oddball in all of sports. With big googly eyes and a wild, orange beard, Gritty is one of a kind.

Gritty made his debut in 2018. At first fans didn't know what to make of this weirdo. Was he a monster? A muppet? But it didn't take long for Gritty to win over fans of all ages. Since then, Gritty has become one of the most popular mascots around.

Gritty really knows how to entertain the crowd. He loves to bust out his dance moves for the fans. And he loves using his t-shirt cannon to blast souvenir shirts high into the stands.

★ STATS ★

**NAME:**
Gritty

**HOME TEAM:**
Philadelphia Flyers

**FIRST APPEARANCE:**
2018

**FUN FACT:**
Gritty was named the league's favorite mascot by NHL players in 2019 and 2020.

# HOWLER THE COYOTE

If you listen closely in the Arizona desert, you may hear the howl of a coyote. It may be Howler, the official mascot of the Arizona Coyotes. He's got big floppy ears and over-sized fangs. But this desert dog won't bite. He just loves to have fun.

Howler wears the number 96. This is a nod to 1996, the year the original Winnipeg Jets moved to Arizona and became the Coyotes. It took a few years for the team to get a mascot. But Howler has been a fan favorite since he first appeared in 2005.

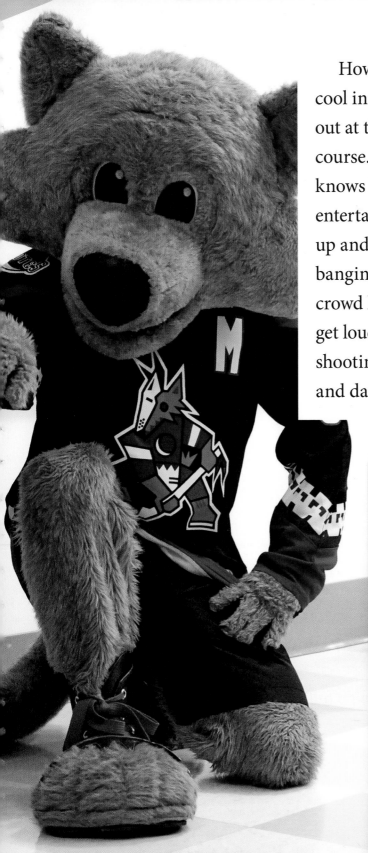

How does this coyote keep cool in the desert? By hanging out at the hockey rink, of course. On game day, Howler knows how to keep the fans entertained. He often marches up and down the stands banging on his mini drum. The crowd knows that's the time to get loud! Howler also has fun shooting t-shirts into the crowd and dancing with the fans.

## ★ STATS ★

**NAME:**
Howler

**HOME TEAM:**
Arizona Coyotes

**FIRST APPEARANCE:**
2005

**FUN FACT:**
Howler's full name is Canis Howlus Maximus.

# YOUPPI

Youppi is hockey's original goofball. With his big orange beard and mustache, he's become a fan favorite. And in 2020, Youppi became the first Canadian mascot to be elected to the Mascot Hall of Fame.

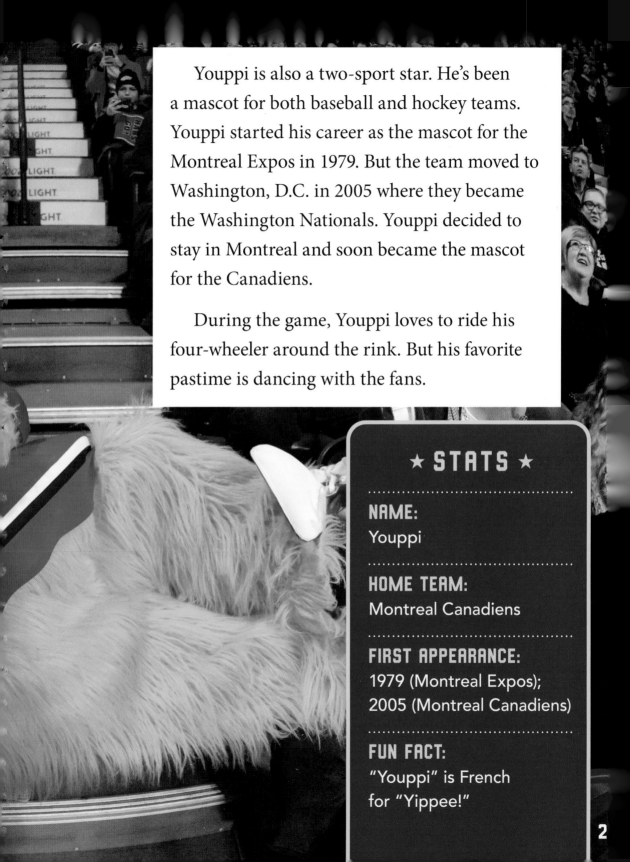

Youppi is also a two-sport star. He's been a mascot for both baseball and hockey teams. Youppi started his career as the mascot for the Montreal Expos in 1979. But the team moved to Washington, D.C. in 2005 where they became the Washington Nationals. Youppi decided to stay in Montreal and soon became the mascot for the Canadiens.

During the game, Youppi loves to ride his four-wheeler around the rink. But his favorite pastime is dancing with the fans.

## ★ STATS ★

**NAME:**
Youppi

**HOME TEAM:**
Montreal Canadiens

**FIRST APPEARANCE:**
1979 (Montreal Expos);
2005 (Montreal Canadiens)

**FUN FACT:**
"Youppi" is French for "Yippee!"

NJ DEVIL

**NAME:**
NJ Devil

**HOME TEAM:**
New Jersey Devils

**FIRST APPEARANCE:**
1993

**FUN FACT:**
NJ Devil's biggest rival is Gritty, the wacky mascot for the Philadelphia Flyers.

## TALL TALES

The New Jersey Devils get their team name from a **mythical** creature. According to legend, the Jersey Devil is a big scary monster that haunts parts of New Jersey. It's supposedly part human and part bird. Stories of the creature have scared kids for decades. There's no proof that the Jersey Devil is real. But it makes for a great mascot.

There's a monster lurking at the ice rink in New Jersey. NJ Devil might be one of the scariest mascots in the NHL. But don't let his appearance fool you. He's nothing but fun.

In between action on the ice, NJ Devil loves to skate around the rink while waving a giant Devils' flag. Seeing the bright red fellow on the ice really pumps up the crowd.

When it's not game day, NJ Devil loves to visit local schools and promote a healthy **lifestyle**. The Devil tells kids to eat healthy and exercise. It's the best way for young hockey players to make it to the NHL!

# MICK E. MOOSE

Mick E. Moose is serious about staying physically fit. He likes to stretch and warm up before each game. All that dancing and high-fiving with the fans can be exhausting!

Like many professional hockey players, Mick E. Moose started his career in the minor leagues. For 15 years, the guy with the big, toothy smile was the mascot for the Manitoba Moose. Then in 2011, he got the phone call all mascots dream about. He was being called up to the NHL!

Mick E. Moose has been the official mascot for the Winnipeg Jets ever since. But he's never forgotten his roots. Sometimes, Mick E. Moose still attends Moose games to cheer on his old team.

★ STATS ★

NAME:
Mick E. Moose

HOME TEAM:
Winnipeg Jets and Manitoba Moose

FIRST APPEARANCE:
1994

FUN FACT:
Mick E. Moose's favorite foods are salads, fruit, and vegetables.

# AL THE OCTOPUS

The Detroit Red Wings are one of the oldest teams in the NHL. They have a lot of **traditions.** One involves the eight legs of an octopus.

In the 1950s, an NHL team needed 8 wins to capture the Stanley Cup title. An eight-legged octopus soon became the symbol of a team's road to the championship. The octopus has been part of the Red Wings team ever since.

**NAME:**
Al the Octopus

**HOME TEAM:**
Detroit Red Wings

**FIRST APPEARANCE:**
1995

**FUN FACT:**
For many years, Red Wings' fans had a strange tradition during home playoff games. They'd throw dead octopuses onto the rink before the game started.

**Did You Know?**

The Detroit Red Wings are one of the "Original Six" teams in the NHL. The other teams included the New York Rangers, Montreal Canadiens, Chicago Blackhawks, Boston Bruins, and Toronto Maple Leafs.

Al the Octopus made his first appearance in 1995. But he's not like other team mascots. Al is a giant stuffed octopus that hangs out in the rafters in the Red Wings' stadium. Before playoff games, Al is lowered to the ice to spin and wave his **tentacles** at the opposing team. The fans go wild for the show Al puts on!

ICEBURGH

Some animals were just made to be hockey mascots. One of them hangs out in Pittsburgh, Pennsylvania. Iceburgh the Penguin is right at home in the chilly ice rink as the mascot for the Pittsburgh Penguins.

Iceburgh isn't the only penguin to root on the team. The Penguin's first mascot was a real-life penguin that first appeared in 1968. It took many more years for the Penguins to get a mascot that could have fun with the fans. Iceburgh made his first appearance in 1992 after the team won back-to-back Stanley Cup Championships.

Iceburgh has been a part of Penguins' home games for 30 years. His dance moves and happy-go-lucky attitude have really won over the fans. One of Iceburgh's favorite moves is to give out some "high flippers" to the fans during the game.

# GLOSSARY

**antennae** (an-TEN-ee)—feelers on an insect's head used for sense and touch

**arena** (uh-REE-nuh)—a large area that is used for sports or public entertainment

**ice age** (EYSS AYJ)—a period of time when Earth was covered in ice

**lifestyle** (LAHYF-stahyl)—a way of living that reflects a person's values, attitudes, and what is important to them

**mythical** (MITH-ih-kuhl)—imaginary or not real

**selfie** (SEL-fee)—a photograph that is taken by the person who appears in it, usually with a smartphone or other digital camera

**souvenir** (soo-vuh-NEER)—an object kept as a reminder of a person, place, or event

**tentacle** (TEN-tuh-kuhl)—a long, armlike body part some animals use to touch, grab, or smell

**trademark** (TRADE-mark)—something that helps identify a company or person

**tradition** (truh-DISH-uhn)—a custom, idea, or belief passed down through time

**Zamboni** (zam-BOH-nee)—a car-sized machine used to clean and smooth the surface of an ice rink

## READ MORE

Davidson, Keith B. *NHL*. New York: Crabtree Publishing, 2022.

Doeden, Matt. *Hockey's Wickedest Goals!* North Mankato, MN: Capstone Press, 2021.

Ellenport, Craig. *Hockey: Score with STEM!* Minneapolis: Bearport Publishing, 2022.

## INTERNET SITES

*Mascot Hall of Fame*
mascothalloffame.com/

*National Hockey League*
nhl.com

*Ranking the NHL's Mascots*
si.com/nhl/2016/10/14/ranking-nhls-mascots

# INDEX

# ABOUT THE AUTHOR

David Carson is a photographer and freelance writer. He's been a sports fan all his life and loves to root on his favorite NHL team, the Chicago Blackhawks.